Contents

Making new plants

Some flowers have more than one colour.

Most plants produce **flowers** every year. Flowers can be lots of different colours. How many different colours can you see in these flowers? Some have more than one colour.

Plants

FLOWERS, FRUITS AND SEEDS

Angela Royston

Heinemann
LIBRARY

First published in Great Britain by Heinemann Library
Halley Court, Jordan Hill, Oxford OX2 8EJ
a division of Reed Educational and Professional Publishing Ltd.

Heinemann is a registered trademark of Reed Educational & Professional Publishing Limited.

OXFORD MELBOURNE AUCKLAND
JOHANNESBURG BLANTYRE GABORONE
IBADAN PORTSMOUTH NH CHICAGO

Designed by AMR Ltd and Celia Floyd
Originated by Dot Gradations, UK
Printed and bound in Hong Kong/China

04 03 02 01 00
10 9 8 7 6 5 4 3 2

ISBN 0 431 00192 8
This book is also available in hardback (ISBN 0431 00186 3).

British Library Cataloguing in Publication Data

Royston, Angela
  Flowers, fruits and seeds. – (Plants) (Take-off!)
  1.Plants, – Juvenile literature 2.Plants – Reproduction –
  Juvenile literature
  I.Title
  581

Acknowledgements
The Publishers would like to thank the following for permission to reproduce photographs:
Ardea: I Beames p10, A Paterson p17; Bruce Coleman Limited: E Crichton p20, G Langsbury
p19; Garden and Wildlife Matters: ppl2, 16,18, 22, 23, 25, M Land p5, C Milkins pp8, 9, J Phipps
p4; Chris Honeywell: pp28, 29; Oxford Scientific Films: H Abipp p21, G Bernard pp11, 26, 27,
D Cooke p13, D Dale p14, C Hvidt p15, D Thompson pp6, 7, I West p24.

Cover photograph: Oxford Scientific Films/H Abipp

Our thanks to Sue Graves for her advice and expertise in the preparation of this book.

Every effort has been made to contact copyright holders of any material reproduced in this book.
Any omissions will be rectified in subsequent printings if notice is given to the Publisher.

For more information about Heinemann Library books, or to order, please telephone +44(0)1865
888066, or send a fax to +44(0)1865 314091. You can visit our website at www.heinemann.co.uk

Any words appearing in bold, **like this**, are explained in the Glossary.

Flowers can be all shapes and sizes. The job of all flowers is to make **seeds** that will grow into new plants.

Different kinds of flowers have a different number of petals.

Buds

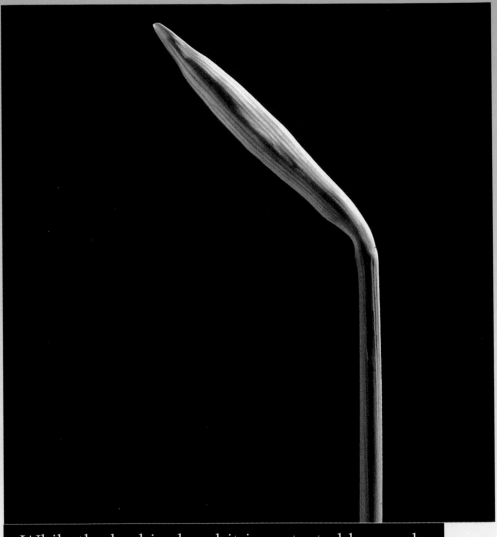

While the bud is closed it is protected by sepals.

A **bud** is a small swollen shoot that grows on a **stem**. All **flowers** begin as a bud. The bud is protected by special leaves called **sepals**.

The bud slowly opens up into a flower.

The sepals slowly unfold as the bud grows bigger. The bud unfolds and opens up into a flower.

Male and female flowers

catkins

This hazel tree produces catkins.

Some plants have two kinds of **flowers**. These catkins are the male flowers of the hazel tree. They make lots of tiny grains of **pollen**.

Many trees, such as willows and birches, produce catkins.

The hazel's female flower is small and hard to spot. Inside the red tips are tiny flower eggs called **ovules**.

The ovules are inside these red tips.

red tip

Grass flowers

grass flowers →

Grass produces green flowers with very light pollen.

Grass has green **flowers** which produce both male **pollen** and female **ovules**.

10

grains of pollen

The wind is blowing this grass pollen onto another flower.

The wind blows the light pollen from one flower onto another flower. When a grain of pollen joins with an ovule, the ovule becomes a **fertilized seed**.

11

Colourful flowers

stamen

style

anther

This colourful flower has both male and female parts.

Many colourful **flowers** have both male and female parts. The male **anthers** are covered with **pollen**. In the middle of the anthers is the female **style**.

The male part of a flower is called the stamen. The stamen is made up of a thin stalk, called a filament, and the anther.

12

Brightly coloured flowers often have a sweet smell. Their colour and smell attract insects that come to feed on a sweet juice called **nectar**.

This butterfly has come to feed on the nectar.

Bees

pollen

anther

Look at the pollen sticking to this bee.

As the bee goes into the **flower** to get **nectar**, grains of **pollen** stick to it. The pollen will rub off onto the **style** of the next flower it visits.

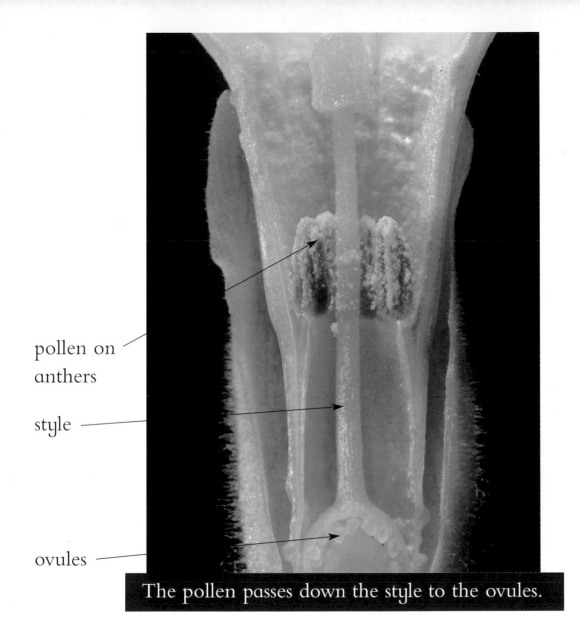

pollen on
anthers

style

ovules

The pollen passes down the style to the ovules.

This marigold has been cut in half to show
the **ovules** at the bottom of the style. Pollen
from another marigold rubs off the bee and
passes down the style to **fertilize** the ovules.

Ripening seeds

cherry
seeds

wilted
flowers

The flowers on this cherry tree have wilted.

Once the **ovules** have been **fertilized**, the petals are no longer needed. They wilt and die. Can you see the wilted flowers on this cherry tree? The cherry **seeds** are beginning to swell.

A juicy **fruit** grows around the cherry seeds to protect them.

These cherries are now ripe and ready to eat.

Birds

seeds

This kiwi fruit has lots of seeds inside it.

Birds help to scatter **seeds**. Can you see the seeds inside this kiwi **fruit**? Birds help to scatter seeds from fruits like this. Seeds grow best if they are scattered far from the parent plant.

When a bird feeds on fruit and berries, the seeds pass through its body and fall to the ground. If a seed falls onto good soil, it may start to grow into a new plant.

This bird likes to feed on ripe, juicy fruits and berries.

Blown by the wind

wing

seed

This tree produces winged seeds.

Many **seeds** are scattered by the wind. Some trees make seeds that have wings. This helps the seeds to blow far away.

Dandelion seeds have little parachutes. They help the seeds to float a long way through the air before they land.

Dandelion seeds have little parachutes of hair to help them float through the air.

Pods

The seeds of peas grow in pods like these.

Some **seeds** grow inside pods. The seeds of peas and beans grow in pods. As the seeds swell, the pods grow longer and fatter.

Plants that grow their seeds in pods are called legumes.

When the seeds are ripe, the pod splits and the seeds are catapulted onto fresh ground away from the parent plant.

Peas can be eaten fresh from the pod.

Nuts

nutshell

A nut is a seed protected by a hard shell.

A nut is a **seed** inside a hard shell. Animals like mice and squirrels bury stores of nuts in the ground. Some of these nuts are not eaten by the animals and grow into new plants.

new palm tree

Palm trees grow from coconuts.

Coconuts grow on palm trees on the beach. When the coconuts fall to the ground, some float out to sea. Some may reach other islands and start to grow there.

A new plant

seed

root

Now the weather is warmer, this seed has started to grow.

Most **seeds** do not grow into new plants. They just die. But this seed has fallen on good soil. It lies in the soil until the weather gets warm enough for it to grow.

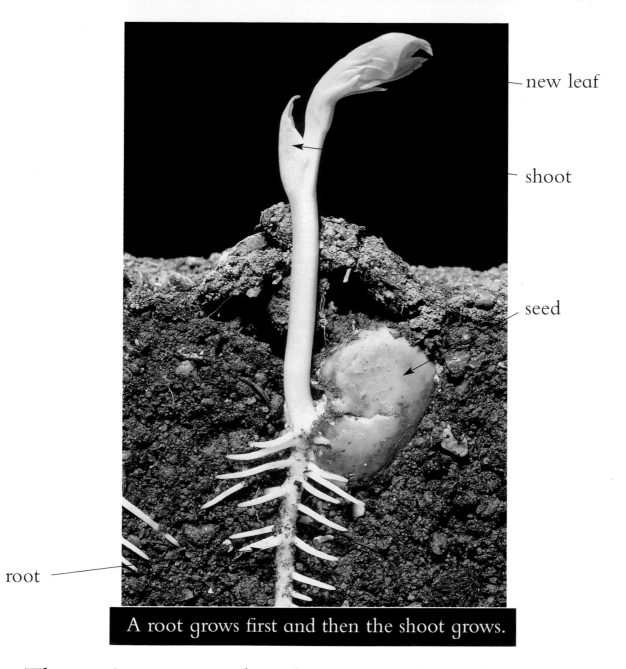

new leaf

shoot

seed

root

A root grows first and then the shoot grows.

The main **root** pushes down into the soil.
Then the shoot starts to grow up through the
soil. More roots grow out from the main root.

Watch it grow

plant pots

damp soil

seeds

It's easy to grow your own sunflowers.

Plant some sunflower **seeds** and watch them grow into **flowers**! You grow them like this:

1 Buy some sunflower seeds from the supermarket.
2 Soak them in water for a day.
3 Plant each in a pot of damp soil.

Don't let your sunflower plants dry out.

4 Leave the seeds until they start to grow.
5 Water the new plants every few days.
6 Keep measuring your sunflower to see how tall it grows.
7 Collect new seeds when the flower dies.

Plant map

A strawberry plant.

leaf

flower

fruit

stem

roots

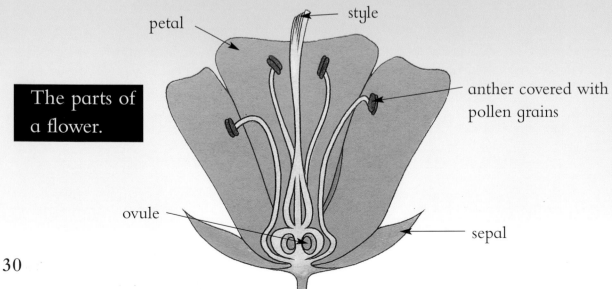

The parts of a flower.

style

petal

anther covered with pollen grains

ovule

sepal

Glossary

anther	male part of a flower that produces pollen
bud	a flower before it opens
fertilize	to make a seed which can grow into a new plant
flower	the part of a plant which makes new seeds
fruit	the part of a plant that holds the ripening seeds
nectar	a sugary juice made by some flowers
ovule	a female seed or egg cell. An ovule must be joined by a grain of pollen to become a fertilized seed
pollen	grains containing male cells which are needed to make new seeds
root	part of a plant which take in water, usually from the soil
seed	a seed contains a tiny plant before it begins to grow and a store of food.
sepal	part of a flower which covers the bud before it opens
stem	the part of a plant from which the leaves and flowers grow
style	female part of a flower which leads to the ovules

Index